THE SUN IS A FAKE REALITY

Vijay Ashok Indushokai

TANEESHA PUBLISHING

ISBN : 9788169244084
Edition : First, March 2026
Title : The Sun Is A Fake Reality (Poetry Collection)
Author : Vijay Ashok Indushokai

Published by

TANEESHA PUBLISHING

An Imprint of **Taneesha and Prachi NextGen Publication**

Registered Office: Sunil Complex, 2nd Floor, Vijay Nagar,
Western Kutchery Road, Meerut - 250002, Uttar Pradesh, India
Website : www.taneeshapublishing.com
E-mail : support@tpnextpub.com
Phone : +91 9760418103

Printed by :
Manipal Technologies Limited, Bengaluru - 560001, Karnataka

The mistake you make, don't you see, is in thinking one can live in a corrupt society without being corrupt oneself.

-George Orwell

To My

Unscattered Firmness and Perpetual Infinity of Self Selfing With All Unself World with Its Selfishness Where Their Fish Never Sell

INDEX

The livings are here the polaritic transgender

The threats of love is the love itself
I hate my love that love itself

The structure of being is being manipulated
I love every instinct and my existence is hated

The livings are here the polaritic transgender
Why shouldn't I expect the world agender

The pollen of humanism should be given to the bees
The world is a lock and pitious are the keys

I pitied myself with hatred cost
I neutralise myself with mindly host

he peace of leaf is a soul of bark

he shadow of dream is a natural scream
sow in the sky and you assume me a meme

he rhythmic chaos is a melody of time
ly frequency of mind is a poetic rhyme

he peace of leaf is a soul of bark
he brightness gets energy from ultimate dark

he anarchy of coincidence is monarchy of being
emocratic principles are dictatorial lying

he dominance of expression is an exploitation worse
he bearers endure it enjoying theological verse

'ou rejoice exploitation with ideological servitude
iscrimination you feel is an existential gratitude

Integrity is falsity of a truthful boast

Why should I record
the particles of life
I usually resonate its fusion
with all possible probabilities

A tired air takes my breath from my mind
I already have displaced my entire being
with anarchic peace

The wholesome is an entity of integrity
Integrity is falsity of a truthful boast
So I believe not in all its binary
and binary-apposition neither

Neither I am hedonic nor sadist
I am the sarcastic of all

I paint my rainbow to the sky of dark

The beams of feelings I preserved into a jar
I polarised my mind to the neutron star

In the well of eyes I fill all solitude
The bubbles of pupil has creative altitude

I paint my rainbow to the sky of dark
They are not only the dogs who generally bark

I lend soil-soul even to mother land
You prejudiced my pity as an inanimate sand

I reside forever in the nucleus of atom
Hearts are never be felt from their bottom

The sun is a fake reality

I need to destroy cocoons of my own
The blank paper is my real autobiography
I read silences of my being

The populated mind I need to perish
because that's not mine at all now

The lines drawn on ocean-water
reflects my unconsciousness

I consciously put my consciousness
into the spark of firefly
The sun is a fake reality

The nights await the perpetuity

The dews of snow I uncovered from Bodhi leaf
The nights await the perpetuity and the universes sleep

The flip of being is an unchanging change
You attempt even emperorly, I am out of your range

The melting point is pointless and the life is Maara
Your real aesthetic you proclaim natural with ideological Mascara

The harmony may harmonious but cruelty is compassion
You declare your falsity, as representation of the nation

It's a hegemonic servitude if consent

I am standing on the edge of honor and dishonor
Why should I believe in karma?
It's a hegemonic servitude if consent

The triviality of jealousy is now materialistic peak
The carcasses of peoples are in the mouth of belief system hyena

I should kill myself for salvation from this stuck world of mire

I can hinge the consciousness to unconscious

The traces of my tears are inevitable
that can unshade the shadow of being
The hazardous life is a stain on existence
I can hinge the consciousness to unconscious
with the ballad of dark and the integral quark

I want to believe at least in nature

I have been preserving monsoon
but my mind didn't get wet yet

The sprinkling splashes of life still stain for me
I want to believe at least in nature
But mostly it seems more unnatural to me

Whether I am in a painting or the paintings are in me?
I am the wormhole of myself

Hued to live

A loved belief system is youth
And then ideological foolishness
hued to live

The innocence in cruelty is
a commercial harmony
to grow economy as the objective

The inevitability of lie
is the truth of the world
And all the cult are life's extensions

The reckons of smells

The reckons of smells are
my equations of golden ratio

The pleasure principles are
valueless and tired
The paranoids are the real braves
And the cowards are the conventional lifers

The crowd of shout is now shout of cry
The feelings emerge are equal to pie
The reality of illusion is now illusion of reality
I am living the past of present
and dimensions of present itself simultaneously

Generally you afraid of them who never afraid of you

I artificially make motherhood

The burden of mind
is the nature of kind
Everything is scattered inevitable
then why should I find?

A found being though integrated
but the essence is there in alienation
The smooth nature is actually interwoven
There is nothing available as perfection

All the antares in the nature
not everytime found natural
I artificially make motherhood

The elixir of death

The elixir of death is an alive life
The fade up servitude is a slavery and life

The bet for liveliness is a deadline flex
The freedom nations neither Oedipus nor Rex

The fleshes of existence are mindly state
Businesses are there with various rate

I auction my essence but her virginity is sold
Everybody knows everything but nobody has told

Others consider me wise

It really sounds good
that I had taken the unwritten social norms otherwise,
otherwise today my perspective might be otherwise for my creativity
though others consider me wise.

Though philosophy is a hypothetical implementation,
Implementation of foolishness is more concrete than the life itself

The civilisation of Earthians

The pathetic fallacy of truth seems truthless everytime
Though
The civilisation of Earthians go ahead

The aestheticism of Narcissists' beauty
must be the lucid dream of nature

I reflect the water into mirrors of life
Though
Life isn't miracast of my being

Time is the mindly dimension of being
The foreseeing of truth is the lie of sight

I allow willow

I allow willow to take my essence from multiverse
It can find all the stages of Bodhisattva of mine there

I can merge the overall realities of all dimensions
for the real truth of timeless time
but time should not be pimp like worlders

The only sleep never makes you sleep
It must be there in DNA to be slave
with all dense shadow and pretending lights

Lights are actually a darkened spark
whose luminous can shine like nights
to bright the real timeline
which never be in line as well

Truth is lying

A crowd fright shrieve to my being
Truth is lying
I am degree nine

The light gives darkness
Sun is manipulated
The world evaporated
I am the dominated

The sun is bastard with valid heir
All knows it’s a reality's affair
Now legitimates should pair

I can grin to the nature

A scratched being can smile
with smashed perspective
I can grin to the nature

The feature that shatter the libido of morality
is a real moral
One can have an ethical sex

My caste is the ghost

The ghosts of mine are my ghosts of life

Past is the ghost

My caste is the ghost

The perpetual discrimination is the ghost

The socio-political structure is the ghost

Only ghosts can live here

The modified and utra-modern ghosts are zombies

I never believe in boast ghost-riders and scientists neither

I hold my breath to grow the sky

The sweat of elixir is a lifely life
It cuts all essence with mindly knife

I sew my heart to keep you in
The mind is logical wants brain to spin

I hold my breath to grow the sky
I want peace of mind and the world says why

The blame on me to accuse myself
You exploit me cruelly and pretend it help

I plough my being for seeds of birds
Freedom will be reaped with revolution of words

Life is never my part

Shadows shiver my heart
Life is never my part

My being is just to be here
It never resembles with here

The language I speak is the language of nothing
The popular language of here doesn't have essence and truthing

Frightenedhood

They expect fear in being
My being is utmost fearless
It eliminates frightenedhood
To make everything no-less

The roaming cowards here pretend to be brave
They about to buy essence but bought a grave

The shave of mountains' genitals for rivers reverie
though sky always falls but mountains want dowry

But lie has dimensional truths

The measures of quality and superiority
is now exploitation mere
Even a lamb should be lion
and its calf should be cub here

Nowadays existence is a game of presumptive assumptions
with its new emerging versions
Truth is not the lie
but lie has dimensional truths
with authentic reality as well

pimp is better than politician

n installed expectation later comes
-built with new generations

waterfall is now barren without losing its aesthetics
can see the helplessness in the eyes of sky

he words never be my autobiographical deeds
he languages now manipulated and hybrid

Yin-yan isn't consisted of two forces
Everything falls under slavery
Breaking it to not to be in is bravery

A pimp is better than politician
Now politicians teach ethics
The manipulators and
Fools are now famous critics

Harmony with prehistoric

The aesthetic brutality of yours,
you proudly feel charity and nonviolent zeal

The match of being and existence should be there in life
Most of the worlders are not of this type

The generality and the nature are now mismatched
with even common sensical sense

The humanistic approach nowadays not humanistic
even it's felt that there was harmony with prehistoric

The only way to live is to leave

The only way to live is to leave
Her presence and smile in my eyes I weave

Let the scattering being be flatter
My words become the cosmic matter

I recite poetry before those
Whose opened eyes are always close

You assume me whatever you want
You expect me to be untrue that I can't

I can weave beauty and smiles

I can weave beauty and smiles
but their essence mostly not real
The oceans might be in their eyes
but eyeless greed is hidden behind

How can I compose the rhymes of fragrance
if flowers are not mine at all
I am not in favor of farming desires
at even the place of micron
though I believe in emotions

I don't want to live in emotions
but want emotions live in me
The displacement and replacement of them
may harm my soul
As I am utmost innocent in this cruel world

Mentality is a dangerous weapon

Evolution of exploitation is technology now
Overconfidence always defeat you from within

Today's life is subsidiary
Mentality is a dangerous weapon

Today's truth is a real truthless

Your lie is the only truth
You believe in

I crystalize my mind

Her perennial quite
Is louder than noise
I am the only deaf
Who can be ruined by voice

I crystalize my mind
To break it into pieces
I repaired my heart
And every moment it greases

Morals destroy innocence
With sacraments and norms
Reality of today is
not in its real forms

I dwell oceans into my pupils

Her melancholy eyes staring a smile
blooming in the mind while
emerging herself into me.

I dwell oceans into my pupils
The beautiful cries of butterflies
become cocoons.

The midst of heart
is my wind of being
Eyes though closed
mind sightseeing

The woods and fire
are from my pyre
Nature tucked up in me
The rivers snuggled to me
I faltered to stifle

My neurons are amateur

The trunks of butterflies
grow into my mind
My neurons are amateur
though they are so kind

I flip my smiles and laughters laugh
My being vibrates I am the half
In my mitochondria Tesseract particles
Humanity reside in universe of parallel verticles

I don't believe in any civilised language.

I elixir my life protecting my mind
with brain's essence
Life has become subsidiary today.
The religion of spirituality is a prostitutional business
There is no spirituality in religion
The hair in my nose should grow natural
Nature is now manipulated
even by natural naturalities as well
I don't believe in any civilised language.

My sleep is an awakeness

When I die in me, I rise
The world is bloody blind, I surprise

though I surprise the fear installed in structure of water
Frequencies manipulated and vibrations chatter

Frequency of my being is core of universe
Galaxies float idle without my cosmic force

My sleep is an awakeness that awakens all
Your civilization rises you think but it’s a fall

Illegitimate truth

I masturbate my mind
The world is over sexual
Morality is the best sexual boast
to conceall pregnant ideologies
to populate the thoughts
thus illegitimate truth
spread to pure the world,
Your manipulation you prove legitimate
in the corrupt court of lie

I am the multi-dimensional mind

When I afraid of words in dream
I wake up to find meaning of mine
I find only blowing sound of brookes
The freedom of sky is one of my
tiny particles of light.

The binary oppositions not merely
opposite to the being,
I fly away my beliefs and ideology
under the earth's sky.

The reality of truth and the
truth of reality both are fake
and pretended to be so.

The delusional illusion always
seen at the seventh and third
degree though, I see it in ninth
degree with all portals of time and being
I am the multi-dimensional mind with all states

A real thought cannot be thought at all

Eying truth cannot be truth
The origin of truth isn't its root
I drain cellulose extracting essence
I won the case but was court of moot
Cunningness is the strength of a coward
Real existence of Earth residents yet to (come) live
Mercy is a merciful pity of self
A real thought cannot be thought at all

Truth-mutants

students are the world itself
They are the learners and the help

They are initiators of the world
The essence of the universe they hold

Though they conceal themselves now
No one can predict when they rock and how

student is an ideology, who break it for need
they are truth-mutants and humanity's breed

can publish the timeline of its anthology

ne elixir is my passion to live.
ne hellish life though has heavenly flowers.
prefer venom of truth to death -alive.

he archaeologists' history of humans is your lie.
know the universal verse of an undiscovered poet.
he only sun you believe Ra is a bastard of your mythology.
can publish the timeline of its anthology.

Pleasure is my inevitable grief

Pleasure is my inevitable grief
My eyes are strong but it's clouds drip

I accept the sky as parachute to joy
It's universe that forcefully to coy

Existences exit into naxystence is grief of glee
Multi verses should be accessible to the elegant flea

The reality of the relation is fake

My objective is to fulfill the objective of the objective
You, the subject deprive all subjection to be subjective

The reality of the relation is fake
Who said to whom to wake

Desired assumptions and expectations are the illusions of truth
The shadows are real and the reality becomes a liar's truth

I am the none

Whatever I am, I am the none
Life's hilarious and its essence's pun

I extract the transcendent's nectar
Universe is a biological pact, I kill the pacter

The science behind science has a sense
The world is scattered, my being is dense

The neurons of heart shies

She mingled into eyes
The neurons of heart shies

Her curly existential libido urges
My being with its essence merges

The lucid of pleasure principle plays
The flowing brookes are actually clays

The physical is meta and
mental is metaphysical
The realities are diseased
and night ain't clinical

The need is love and
the pleasure is spiritual
Yin yang pretends to be contradict
Their existence is a real mutual

I crumbled my petals

I crumbled my petals
Because to love fragrances
Though the sun seems darkened
Before my essence

I eradicate the fools and they kept their falsity
A dragonfly is caught by a flower
I am human and there is humanitarian scarcity

I blast the brook of pain

I blast the brook of pain
I burst its origin, the centre of eye
I am the farmer, who yields through rye
The fortitude is immoral for the moral lie
The pristine petals are whore you call

I am the Acrylic

Need has hues
and shades
I am the green
though she has reds
I am the Acrylic

Sky is black
I hole it blue
My mind is leak
I apply there glue

Nature reside in me

The thorns languish for my tear
I can comprehend the thirst of nature
A lake makes though mind mindful
but its leaking heart brookes through my veins

A breeze essences my being
though the beauty of sun-set never sets in my mind
I can rise thousand sun-rises from my blood
because I am there in every particle of it

Nature resides in me and my mind is an ocean
I cannot blink the days and nights
Every moment live me in nature
The blade of a grass is my pass to enter
into being as being myself

I am the only banker

I sit beside a pond
frequently looking at
its still whispering water

The flowers never bank
never be deposited to save
I am the only banker

The wild fragrance makes me
conscious sometimes
When pond sat beside me
I never realize to know
my fragrance of nature

Now the whispering water
still in my mind with all essences
and with all perpetual memories

In every monsoon, the pond sprouts in my mind
The ecology creates the worlds within
I fly there as butterfly and firefly

Now their pyres smell

The musical Banyan leaves
and serene Bodhi leaves
can listen the rhymes of my heart

The soul of the soil within me can grow the woods
My morrow is generating the cruds

The sunset I languish for is still in my iris
I can clutch the neurons of my memories
to be indigenous of land

The Nilgiri trees witnessed my adolescence
The fragrance of Nilgiri leaves extract from my being

The smooth grass and hard log of trees
never manipulated essence of my adulthood

The rivers were my beloved
Later it were decorated as divine-mother
Now their pyres smell

Now it seems imperial

I can stretch my childhood
for the company of river
River used to hug me entire day
with ultimate warmth
The very smell of river
sticked to my being

I used to catch fish
as if river provoke me so
There is no discrimination in nature
in any form nor rules there
Nature is just nature like
nothing and everything that's all
My hunger of life is its part
River was like mother but
now it seems imperial

.t the same time

.t the same time childhood
s well as old age is being lived by
.t the same time life as well as death chases each-other
.t the same time yin-yang meets to mingle into
.t the same time mind and heart fuck me as a being of existence
.t the same time universe melts into me and I am dissolving into it
.t the same time time is timeless and is rigid and delusional
.t the same time agender is emerging into sexes
nd cell division stops at one
.t the same time vibrations become wave and vise versa
.t the same time everything is nothing and nothing is thrice versa with all
imensions
.t the same time multiverse is a poor lane and spread all over the infinity
.t the same time I am not myself

I dip myself in dews to reap

My sorrow fulfill its thirst at the lake of scorch
The blossoms in my mind is in very middle march

The pleasure principle of life evocates being as existence
The essences got manipulated and pure nothing becomes nayxistence

I dip myself in dews to reap
The confinement of being I have to keep

The rain sprouts in me to yield my souls
I am the purposeless then why there are goals

I slide on question marks to mark them
Life is trivial and it is a gamble game

Logic is the key

The rose petals in nectar with penetrate spark
A skinned sandal hypocrite and the original is bark

The serpent locked an existential bell
The world pretends heaven though it's more than hell

The tender buds crumbled by the pimps
"It's social hierarchy", said the blimps

The rote morals languish for sipped ethical
You are making real life the bloody mythical

The controlled consciousness conscience everything
Logic is the key, unlocking truth of everything

The organic lie and hybrid truth

A hegemonic truth is a hypothetical boon
The bloody anarchic are now in cacoon

The organic lie and hybrid truth
The blinds want it as life smooth

The skyish boast boosts at land
Diamonds are futile and valuable sand

Mirages are real oceans of your world
How could I explain truth who are already fold

My cruelty was kind

My childhood spreads in river
I hold nostalgia for its cover

The innocence and emotions confluence
I was my philosopher with all influence

My fears, my doubts become my guide
My naked existence was wild though I never hide

My cruelty was kind and no one was blind
I killed my subject-formation with soul to grin

Childhood and old age are two banks of the same river
I sank to bath in freezing cold though never shiver

I slice myself into tiny billion parts

I have to incomplete my completeness
The summer-absurd is my being- base

I slice myself into tiny billion parts
Every part has minds and all have the heart

I am the nothing with all being essence
The presence is actually the only absence

I pour my intestine with syenite dart
The sun is nothing but left over kart

The galaxies I spite can heal the universe
The bloody human beings are nothing but curse

'hough you know my caste

tied my knot to brook and wind it into heart
'he sky sips me up though it is my tiny part

'he very fragrance of soil is soul of nature
ocieties are always uncivilized and cruel butcher

rhymed my mind for a rhythmic heart
eaves spiritualize being with lifely dart.

motional-weave is a skit of birds
olitude-nothing is my living swords

he hues know me are betrayal past
am the casteless though you know my caste

I travel through neurons in multiverse

A being of glass cracked in me
The grief is broken and comes glee

The days and nights all galaxies are fake
Universe is sprouting from me and all I make

I spray myself on the stained innocence
The reality is false though has reputance

I break cocoons of sky
the omnipotence is the only lie

I travel through neurons in multiverse
Words should not be in neither verse

The liquid of sun

I am the Narcissus of the true world quest
my water has been flown, nothing is rest

I bend the gleam with the liquid of sun
I surpass all consciousness and the unconsciousness blown

The energy that I feel a realization of truth
The untrue attracts polarities become smooth

The aim is aimless and it is at all
Living is nothing but a spam missed call

Lie is the only truthful boast

A crying pleasure mourns the glee of grief
You can take my life's account in a brief

A caged freedom is liberty of servitude
It's a pretended truth that you will see as your attitude

Lie is the only truthful boast.
The bank of the desert is now the real coast.

The I know is a foe of truth
cruel harmony with pity is a lovely-ruth

Criminals are rivals and ideal of tort
Democracy's holocaust is salvation and civil life is bart

I leak the universe up to thrice

My trunk of being seeks flowers
Antenna in mind with brainily towers

I minimize the world within my eyes
I leak the universe up to thrice

The lava-nectar I preserve in hive
Why should I think of this world to dive?

A hollowed sun

Pleasure is mine
now calamity glee
sorrowful flea
flies not.

I made taboo
to my please
worldly cease
still continues

I bloom happiness
and peace within
The real within
Outsider

A hollowed sun
faster than run
my lifely pun
is pun not

Illusions are now
real authentic
mine antique
unnoticed

Revisiting my being

Revisiting my being is a frequent life
And
The happiness isn't real,
You have created an illusion of happiness
to conceal your boast and its cruel grief

The imagination of the era can be the fact of generation
But still my essence remain essential and authentic real
Now I don’t believe in the world and life they call
I reboot my existence

The Shadow is a Realistic Fake of Pleasureful Glee

Sun is always behind

He cannot appear identically at all
As the bright sun is always behind
She has been nurtured as worth
that he is the only extremely kind

Her childhood memories and fantasies contradict
Though she managed with her being under sacrament
She used to feel liberal and free at all
but inside her there are growing woods of confinement

Her existence is in shadow as she is taught
She is persuaded for all discrimination as reality
In spiders' webs she is systematically caught
She has been living in the real fake reality

Your sun rises in your reality only

The shadow you bestow happiness
is your nest of dark
The sun light you believe
will never spark

Your sun rises in your reality only
where the real reality never rise
You propagate that your voice is heard
Then how the deafs listen to your voice

Your reality is the only hallucination
and your servitude is your freedom realization
Asking question is ban in your civilisation
You feel honored though you know this notion

Her life is now lighter than light

A very innocent girl asked, why sun rises
Granny said a mythological story of man
Then she asked why sun is a man
Granny convinced her the importance of his clan

The tales and folklores she believes
And belief system becomes her reality
Her subject subject formation, fate she believes
Everything is normal she feels even cruelty

Her life is now lighter than light
She kites her being more than kite
The dark for her is whiter and white
Her eyes are now the object and sight

The sun is white

People flow darkness as the radiant
Their being is not being though they believe
Weaving roots of life in soil should relieve

Time waits for light and shadow
Shines there though it's black-widow

You can play the playings of your play
The sun is a fake reality though you slay

The rhymes music knows may be rhythm
You pretend servitudes the real freedom

The sky is not blue and oceans dead
The sun is white and the world's trade

Sleeping hands' may slip the mind
Your motor is faulty, let me wind

The day is night

The eyes are light
and perspectives night
your darkened essence
you feel it's bright

You are happy for
materialistic spirituality
All desired- Peace of mind
is a qualityless reality

The day is night
with dense and fog
The woods brighten
though lit not log

Nights sleep in him

He sleeps in night
and nights sleep in him
you are extra-ordinary
and the real-truth whim

He is the words
of your language
Helpless humanity
is compared with gauge

The bundle of thread
mingled in-within
Your Life and its meaning
now not in-within

Flowers are death

The words are sewing
the broken sun
stitches of mind
are conscious none

The oxymoron pun
is a metaphor of life
Flowers are death
and immortality is knife

She compares her grand-daughter
to the fragrance of flower
Her daughter is fascinated
to the ultimate sun shower.

Cannibalism is festival of rich

A sophisticated teen throws
an illegitimate baby girl
she was conscious about
and totally not whirl

cruelty is normal in civilization
cannibalism is festival of rich
Though their religion contradict
Religions suck blood,
are for humanity leech

The devotees of sun
may sun of bitch
Animals converted into humans
though they cannot switch

A tearing tear

A tearing tear
of seven years girls
who is tore
by religious whores

The parents of girl
could see her face
They were enjoying
her ruin without stress

A stale mentality
that rotten their soul
Their essence decay
with an existential hole

The arsefucker and cowards

Your superstitious truth
is a rotten gold
An ash- empires within
you always hold

The truth you proposed
is not even thing
The ethical morals
from where you bring.

The parasites you believe
a divine deity
The arsefucker and cowards
you feel mighty

He lays eggs to eat

He lays eggs to eat
Her existence is nothing
but for him a fresh meat

He is the colossus cultured
and is prestigious in society
His popularity is honored though vultured

Your pride, your civilization
everything is just bullshit
When will you get this realization

A boy is raped

A boy is raped
In his mind a cage is kept

He wants to fly with cage
For flying outside, societies always amaze

He believes in his mother a lot
so didn't able to remove the navel knot

His mother is socio-religious puppet
Existential essence and innocence snippet

His beliefs, his mind and existence fuse
He is a divine said religious muse

His mother fought his father to offer him to god
society enforce him to accept fate and think broad

The Rhyme of Truth is Reality-Rhythm
The World is Trap though you call it Freedom

Fireflies are more than your the sun

You project hope to desperate it
Hope is the only tool to be slave
you call pessimism disquality
because it leads towards truth and liberty.

You sustain your boast at any cost.
though the empires and civilizations lost
your superstructure's base is on
the sleazy dung

Fireflies are more than your the sun
you torch darkness in real light
you afraid to the real authentic
light

His hate will sprout lovely affinity

The birth of his poems
are on the death of his desires.
The blood of his soul
waters your soil

He hates your damn civilization
which is inhumane and pitiless
to love the modified harmonious humanity
His hate will sprout lovely affinity

He wants to change all connotations
that corrupt the languages and dialects
He is weaving the fresh flowers
in language whose fragrance can
emerge novelty and creativity
with unimaginable imagination
for real reality of truth

You may believe in poetry

The narrations, metanarratives of
their lives mean not what they live
An unknown narrator also unknown
to all the facts and realities

One cannot be the one to know
what everyone should know

The ears and the anecdotes
with mouthpiece of stories
can inherit truth
but cans are used to preserve liquor
not to be fully conscious about.

You may believe in poetry
if you want to see the
transparent sun rays of the
world to conceal truth.

The rays of hope

When his girl was killed then his wife killed the killer
and called him eunuch

His identity and his reality both are different
He does not believe in contradiction
while she lives reality with possibilities

He accepts her after girl's death
but lane and clan ask him to prove his manliness

After a month his wife's dead body found in saw mill
marked with saw chain

He remarries a girl to start his new life
with all the hopes and the rays of hope
on which the world is sustained

An innocent lamb

An innocent lamb writes history of jungle
The hero was ram and ship
who hunt tigers and lions

Eagles serve them with loyalty
They cut their wings to show loyalty

Hyenas are the only trustworthy and cultured creatures

Now the only lamb is ruling jungle
as his ancestors dead in Pandemic

As an emperor, lamb wants to kill prestigious rabbit
who initiates depopulation program
but his ministry oppose him

He is frightened by a conspiracy
that can snatch his throne.

He is safe now ignoring
all the realities of the jungle

His expectation is that
the jungle should save him
although the entire jungle be ruined

She is no more to forgive anyone

She decides to be piteous towards all
She forgives everyone and everything of everyone

An adolescent molested her
She got furious
So that boy beg her then she forgives him

The boy makes plan
He gang raped her
with his friends and murdered her

She is no more to forgive anyone

Now invisible like justice

A builder crushed the entire slum area
Thousands of poor people died
One minute tv news, headlines in newspapers
A topic of gossip for some people to pass time
Formal sympathy some where
Some government and non-government institutions,
associations get benefit

One social media handle shout a lot for justice
One poet writes poem on them
They both of them are now invisible like justice

His untouchable being

His poverty never allow
him for romantic love
with the realities of his fantasy

Nights; particularly power cut one
gratify him
The continues noise of cricket's love
and summer-hot jerk him off

His untouchable being never
touched and being
His flowing adolescence
always blew

He pales for the ideological
notion of civilization
that's love
because of the same
civilizational ideology
that's idealism

He lost his natural
existence for idealism
that later proved futile.

Real truth is yet to reveal

What will he do with all pleasures
that are mortal and troublesome

His fantasies and fallacies
he live immortal
but the interpretations of dreams
and their reality is his grief

He hates reality
He hates society
because for society he is lower caste

He knows he can change reality
but the economic reality is harnessed
with social ideologies towards him

He hates belief systems
of civilization and its truth
because the real truth is
yet to reveal

He lures for uppercaste girl

He lures for uppercaste girl
Once he stares her in weekly local market
she is being pushed on him
Her breast touched his palm
He preserved his palm as memory of her
He famoused for cutting palm
upper caste people murdered him
They burnt his entire family outskirt
Organizations protest
but no one give justice to the ash
as well.

The temple is in profit

The novel feelings of a teen are manipulated by a priest
she was raped by him with hymn

He made her believe that
she becomes pure after virginity breaks
She doesn't even know what virginity is

He is the son of
the former temple priest of a village.
Both, oldie and young
taste about all the village
girls except the girls of
their community

The temple is in profit
the priests are happy
that's why the village
is prosper even in
this 21st century.

I fuck your bloody morals and ethics

Your rotary sins you assume virtues
I fuck your bloody morals and ethics
your contradictory civilization I jerk off

As a human being you are flop
though you pretend to be
savior of humanity

Your inhumane deeds are
utmost cruel and even more
than any comparison

I condemn your bloody existence

If you assume freedom to servitude?

A coconut is baking in the scorching sun
The water inside is semen you say
and ask virgin to eat to be pregnant
as your mythological technologies say

You believe in illogical magic
with unscientific logic

Your entire existence you
make lie without any shy
you pride on your ancestral slavery

How can I free you
if you assume freedom to servitude?
You eyes are inside
as the action of ostrich

Your attitude is your dirtitude
and perspective is darkened within

Unmasking the Masquerade Realities to Naked the Nudity as well

Your civilization is a masquerade

You fucked nature cruelly
now nature will fuck you
No one, never be saviour

Lights never lit for light
Now sun wants to be unmasked
your civilization is a masquerade

your existence is nayxistence of none
you can prove anything to prove
to be proved the proof.
A lie never becomes true.

Your humanity is a living cementery

The aesthetics you create
naked not the truth
your nudity doesn't have aestheticism

You decorate vulgarity as art
your art is artless and null
You cannot conceal your reveals

Water is water of nature
and the water you made is
a transparent dead
Your humanity is a living
cemetery with burial pun

Exclusively excuse of the bright sun

He lives his versions ahead
to be nostalgic
He was she and she was they
to be human being
All should be all and the null

The reality of the sun is assumed
presumptive realities are falser than lie
The sky desired to be grazed in human beings

The universe is synchronized in our eye
There is huge difference between perspective and the real eye
Her innocent pre-teen mind adapted
the exclusively excuse of the bright sun

For your renowned puerile

They ripe the mind of soil
She never remains the unripe sound
Frequencies he emits are cosmic nerve

The follies are aged and buds die early
The pastures erode the skin of sky
The wind is winded with the woven water

You play the game of crown
as being a clown
Your opposition work
for your renowned puerile
People are fool with the foolest zeal

Dragonfly and soul both are foul

The very relation between is always relationless
Pollen is the only link between nature and life
Aquarium is never about water
while barter system is only living

Dragonfly and soul both are foul
if life is not a fame of game
The game of the game never seems game
You are bloody gambler who never win

he is what that you never think

he poets' words and
ıeir meanings of you never resemble
er beauty is clock and time is lock
he is what that you never think
ıd vise and thrice versa

e born for languish and diminish
ɔmetimes to innovate and create
ıe recreation of novelty to change the existents

hey blame to believe
ıd believe to blame
he claim is proclaim
hey are always they are
om ancient times
ith upgrades of slavery

Poets are theft

Poets are theft who steal every arbitrary
from all dimensions even the time
Their free verse is hymn
and sonnets crime
to justify even with poetic justice

He revives Tukaram, Jotiba Phule,
Babasaheb Ambedkar
and Namdev Dhasal

She revives Savitrimai Phule,
Mukta Salave and Arundhati Roy

Though they follow the arsefuckers dead
who pretend to be alive to kill them all

Them are less to fool

They murdered their 'I' under cultural hegemony
They accept their soul to be manipulated for momentary things
They engulfed by the idealism of the them
Idealism is one of the powerful tools to make commons slave like hope

The difference between they and them is different
They are in mass number and them are less to fool
Some they know although they are under the influence of them

The politics and diplomacy between they and them is very political
Now bio-psychological geology has been sustained by them with manipulation legacy of cruel-pity with violent-harmony and inhumane-humanity being passed through tales, mythology, folks, language, dialects, recipes and cultures

She fed her mascaraed breast

An innocent child plays in park
She was very happy with her widowed mother
Her father was sacrificed for country
He was in army
Suddenly the child burst
as a bomb attacked by foe country
Her mother was shocked,
was alive little bit

Her upper body was remain
Her daughter's head bounced to her
She fed her massacred
breast to the head and died

After some years
both the countries reunited
and become friends
with treaties and compromise

Now she fixed her father-fixation

Her first menstrual cycle
and her family's religious legacy
made her guilty of being a girl.
Her girlhood is the sin.

She is logical and scientific approach
She always question everything
even the existence

She is Gen Z with her eight years old sister
She is always badly beaten by her father
with his traditional eye
Her psychological being is castrated

Now she fixed her father-fixation
throwing electra complex into the dust bin

Is he a coward or is society sterile?

Now he fears to be loved
even though it comes from family
Is he a coward or is society sterile?

He is neither frustrated nor depressed
His status is very high in society
But he hates it with its civilization

Is he abnormal or the society is diseased
Is civilization deceased or is he alive?
Now it's your obligation to be neutral
or to be a real humanitarian?

His calm resonates him every moment

How a father surpasses the pure emotions
of his daughter towards a cruel dog?

He wants to respect her teenage feelings
to be fulfilled as her sweet memories of life
but it may be corrupted in today's world.

He cannot want to make her to bury
her nostalgia in further life.

Her innocence restricts him to restrict her
but restrictions are trivial than harm
His calm resonates him every moment

India is the hub of everyday Epstein files

A very theist seeks a new born girl in hospital
with dark eye to gratify his god

His eyes were blue, he was fair and stall
He feels himself innocent and loyal to religion

Finally he got a baby girl in government hospital
with help of nurse and doctors

The baby first cries a lot then stares at him and smile to laugh
She sucks his finger as she was hungry whole day

He puts her before deity, does some ritual
She starts crying aloud as she holds the flame of lamp

A loud sound is there and her voice stops
He takes her heart out,
which is still beating outside,
tears tore from open eyes
He drags out both her dense eyes with joy

He considers a divine sage in theological society
now as he completes the target of one hundred and eight

India is the hub of everyday Epstein files

Agender can uproot your all systems

Antisociopathic neurology you weave amongst them with systematic nerve
Their basic physical, emotional, social, status needs are their foes

Agender can uproot your all systems
that you incepted into their mitochondria
Transgenders will transcivilise your bloody civilization you proud of

Your eternal sun is the son of whore
Everyone will drink water full to pour
The ashes will wet to spoil in dark
Your shadows will also be tore

They definitely will

The noises you heard to ignore
are the voices of them
They directly mention you not as imperial but a trivial

Your power structure is powerless
until they are responding you
otherwise your existence is in minus of nayxistence

They have to be more aware, awakened,
conscious and united with one linearity
and they definitely will